Christina, 7/26/20

the
WORLD
is
BETTER
WITH
in it

Hope you
enjoy this
BOOK.

Re-Mind Me

Re-Mind Me

by Ole Dammegård

Int. Raya Yoga Teacher

*With eternal gratitude to the
Light of my Life & my daily Inspiration;
Kim "Kamala"*

The intent of the author is only to offer information of general nature to help you in your quest for emotional and spiritual well-being. In the event you use any of the information in this book for yourself, which is absolute right, the author and the publisher assume no responsibility for your actions.

ISBN: 9781790115983

Cover design by Ole Dammegård
Title inspired by Dora
Copyright © 2010 Ole Dammegård
Second Edition 2018

Contents

Foreword

By Nalanie Chellaram
International Raya Yoga Teacher

Many of us are plagued with emotions such as fear, guilt, worry, greed, jealousy etc, that make us feel very uncomfortable. It is vital that we confront these issues logically and deal with them. If we don't, they will constantly take control of our lives.

We are given the intelligence to decipher our thoughts and emotions. But how many of us actually take the time or make the effort to do so? Thoughts make up a person and thoughts have amazing powers. With the practice of Yoga one is taught to discipline and harness the thought waves. Our minds are like computers and we need to be strong enough to input positive data to sublimate and destroy viruses.

Through knowledge and meditation, one can grow to understand one's emotions and generate them positively so that an easeful, peaceful and useful life can be lived. Life is short so we need to use our time efficiently and happily.

Understanding that we all come from the same source dilutes the selfish ego and takes us to a new paradigm of compassion, love and service.

When that happens an inner glow enters our being making our outer world into a heaven. As we think, so we become, so it is.

Ole Dammegård has put this dynamic manual together to illustrate how life can be lived to its fullest. There is no judgment, no plan, just a road map to guide us to exist in this world with the highest spiritual understanding.

His aim is to provide this wonderful knowledge to serve others who find the traditional approach too difficult to understand. Ole has gone through the spectrum of life's obstacles and sufferings and has emerged not only unscarred or bitter, but full of love and gratitude.

May this booklet serve many on their path to Self–realization. May many be inspired to live a spiritual life in this earthly body and fill the world with peace and joy.

In 1986 Nalanie Chellaram formally became a disciple of His Holiness Sri Swami Satchidananda. She has since then been accredited by the Council of Teachers of the Satchidananda Ashram in Virginia, USA. She is also an accredited Teacher Trainer for Integral Yoga and a therapist under the British School of Yoga.

She is currently Chairman of the Integral Yoga Centre in Gibraltar as well as the Founder of the www. SISproject.org. In 2008, Nalanie received a medal of honour from Queen Elizabeth for her "Services to Humanity".

Welcome to the game *'My Life'*, also popularly known and referred to as *'Re-Mind Me'* or *'Dissolving the Matrix'*. In this short manual we will outline the basic rules of this universal game. We will also give some indications and useful tips on what to do and what not to do.

NO RIGHT OR WRONG

In this game created in a virtual reality nothing is right or wrong, all events are just based on cause and effect.

The designer of the game is not interested in passing judgement on how it is being played. He is only interested in upholding the balance of 'life'.

And even though the game may look and feel very real, it is all just an illusion.

The player is neither his Body nor his Mind but the immortal self playing a wonderful game with itself.

To create adventure and excitement, duality has been added as well as a special team of Black Angels (a software installed to keep the player in the dark). These Black Angels are sometimes referred to as the 'bad guys'.

FIND THE WAY BACK HOME

The main task for the player is to solve and pass as many tests as possible, while trying to find his way home (returning to his origin).

This can be accomplished in a myriad of ways (truth is one, paths are many) by choosing whatever combination of levels the player finds most entertaining.

Many obstacles will be put in the way to develop and fine-tune the player's skills and test his perseverance and courage. The progress and development of the game therefore depend on the player's willingness to understand and become the master of his mind.

A multitude of other online players will come and go on the main stage which is projected on the player's digital 3D screen (the world as we know it). The dynamic interaction with these players will create whatever situation the player would like to learn from.

The level of difficulty will be based on the player's earlier games and accomplishments (karma), on a scale from 1-10: 1 = An ant, 10 = A highly evolved human being.

Please keep in mind: The player will always be totally safe, taken care of and guaranteed to 'win' the game in the form of enlightenment; it is just a matter of when and how. The main challenge is to uncover that it is all just a divine Joke, a trick of light where nothing is real. And if you shouldn't succeed the first time, don't worry - be happy. There are plenty of opportunities to play the game (reincarnation).

Only one thing is required: you have to practise for a long time, without a break and with all your heart. And so the big game begins ;-).

BODY AND MIND

The Body (the computer) and Mind (the communication system) are the vehicles through which the player can 'physically' experience this illusion of reality.

The body has been equipped with 2 types of memory, the RAM (the subconscious controlling bodily functions, etc) and the processor (the brain) for calculating and solving tasks and equations.

AN ILLUSION

The mind will give the player the false experience of time, form and space. And his 'body' is merely a residual-self image, the mental projection of his digital self.

This means that the 'physical' world the player sees as outside himself only exists in his mind. Actually, he is not seeing at all, instead his eyes are being used as projectors sending his manifested thoughts into so called 'reality'.

In the same way, his body is not really breathing, it is being breathed. Just like he is not actually thinking.

This is mainly being done by the motherboard, which controls most basic functions and also generates a steady stream of some 60 000 thoughts per day.

So what appears to be 'real' is electrical signals interpreted by the player's brain, into a neural-interactive simulation or a computergenerated dream world.

The player's responsibility is to choose which thoughts to amplify and give power, thus creating his future.

All impressions of sight, smell, sound, touch and taste are equally false, just being waveforms decoded into virtual reality through the graphic card and the sound card, etc.

CREATE A PERSONAL CHARACTER

Before starting a new game (being born), the player needs a computer (the body) to be able to play. The next step is to go online on the Internet (the matrix).

He is then asked to create an account (his identity). Once logged in, the player can start to create his own personal character, with which he will be playing the game.

Here he is offered a wide range of character types, such as, for example:

Drama queen, victim, bully, rebel, hero, leader, follower, warrior, addict, etc. He can also choose from a selection of pre-made memory banks to add to the spectrum and adversity of duality.

More advanced players who easily get bored have got the possibility to choose among additional plug-ins (traumas).

The variety of character types and situations are essentially made to create an exiting feature called problems (challenges to be solved, thus adding achievements such as better understanding, empathy and added skills).

BACKGROUND THEMES

The player is then allowed to select background themes, like century and part of the world, war or peace, length of lifetime as well as additional online characters like family, close friends, acquaintances, foes and enemies.

The player can even choose gender, general appearance, hair colour, body type, skin colour, birth date, sexual preference and religious faith. In addition the player can choose his:

- Level of intelligence, on a scale 1-10
  (1 = Brain dead, 10 = Genius)
- Level of wisdom, on a scale 1-10
  (1 = Ruthless serial killer, 10 = Saint)

CHAOS FACTOR

Once all the major selections have been made, the final combination is put through an advanced mathematical process called the Mysterious Chaos factor.

When this is done, the player will be equipped with a totally unique personal character consisting of an amazing blend of individual features.

THE EGO

To make the game last as long as possible, it is essential to keep vital information hidden from the player.

The game designer has accomplished this by installing special software (the ego) causing the player to forget his true self thus starting to believe in separation and abandonment.

This is done in combination with shutting down nine tenths of the brain's capacity, more specifically the parts that are connected with the divine.

From now on, the ego will do everything to trick the player into thinking that he actually IS the body/mind.

EMOTIONS – THE INDICATORS

Emotions are then added as subtle indicators, helping the player to stay on the 'right path'.

Feelings of anger, guilt, hatred, frustration, irritation and despair are clear indicators that the player is going the wrong way, whereas feelings of love, compassion, forgiveness and empathy show him that the correct way is being followed.

Another good indicator of how to play the game in the most beneficial way is to follow the basic rule:

- Selfish actions are painful
- Selfless actions are painless

SILENT VOICE

All along a 'Silent Voice' in the player's mind will offer wise advice on how to play wisely. Most new players make the mistake of ignoring this subtle voice, which most often results in hard lessons to learn.

Another thing to watch out for is a cleverly designed plug-in called shyness, which will disguise itself as something very good and adorable, but is actually a product of the ego, installed to slow down the player.

BRAIN WASHING

One of the first levels is called growing up. Here the player has to go through a process called School education, where the player's processors are being filled up with seemingly important but mostly useless information.

This is supplied to cause distraction and confusion thus aiming at tricking the player to forget his true self (brain washing).

COMFORT ZONE

The player is finally programmed to believe that he is all alone, mortal and separated from the other players and the Source.

Without this belief (something repeated but often not true), the game could not continue so, most of the time, the player is being bombarded with false information. This is done through media and other players like parents passing on traditions and their own fears, in this way trying to keep the player as inactive as possible.

An additional plug-in is then installed creating the so-called comfort zone, adding to the false importance of not challenging anything new.

ATTACKED BY THE OPPOSITE

Should the player decide to ignore this and decide to try out new levels, he will immediately be challenged from all directions, the reason for this being a strong attempt to force him back into the comfort zone.

The weapons used against him will often take the shape of the exact opposite of what the player is trying to achieve.

In addition, some players will have to pass the hormonal and challenging process of replicating (having children); and for the female players the somewhat feared time of men-onpause (menopause), a mirrored process of being a teenager.

BEING BOMBARDED – A GOOD SIGN

In other words, if for instance the player would like to change body type, let us say from fat to fit, the player will now be bombarded with negative thoughts and impressions about why 'this is impossible' to accomplish.

Most players will succumb to this pressure, but more advanced players might be able to see this as a great sign indicating that he is on the right path and close to accomplishing his goal.

So if he corrects his mind, everything else will most likely start falling into place.

THIS TOO SHALL PASS

In turbulent and seemingly difficult situations it is therefore recommended that the player focus on peace while repeating the words "This too shall pass, this too shall pass".

By doing so, the player will be reminded that nothing last forever and that he will always be safe. Soon he will have passed the invisible borders of the comfort zone and is then allowed to continue on his way.

That is, of course, until he decides to face new challenges.

ONLY TWO OPTIONS

When confronted with any type of situation or problem, there are basically only two options to choose from: Love or Fear. The two cannot co-exist. All other feelings are just variations.

- Fear will stop the flow and the progress
- Love will solve any type of problem and get the player back in the flow

There are endless variations of handling the often difficult interaction with other players. To make the game flow as easily as possible, here are some general guidelines and attitudes to cultivate:

- Friendliness towards the happy
- Compassion for the unhappy
- Delight in the virtuous
- Disregard towards the wicked

DELETE PATTERNS

Once a major problem has been solved, the player is allowed to continue for a certain amount of time, before being confronted by the problem once more (often in a less dense form).

A pop-up will then appear on the player's screen, saying: "Are you sure you want to delete this behaviour / situation?" The player can now click 'Ok' or 'Cancel.'

- Clicking Ok will delete this type of situation, once and for all.

- Clicking Cancel will make the situation re-appear in new forms and shapes, until the player is content and decides to let it go.

Please note: Some tasks might take time to solve and demand a lot of courage and strength since there is always the option of:

- Striving upstream by struggling very, very hard (the ego's way)

or

- Relaxing and flowing downstream (going with the divine will and effortlessly follow the river towards the source)

CREATE CONSCIOUSLY

Another major task is figure out how to create consciously. This is being hidden and only shown to devoted searchers of the truth.

But in this basic manual we have decided to give new players a few hints:

To create anything new, just send out a rocket of desire, and then add a high emotion to access the same vibration as the goal to be manifested.

Repeated thoughts create form, but the Feeling is the real key to be able to manifest successfully.

This is, however, easier said than done, since a dose of amnesia is being pumped in every time a player seems to have understood the plot of the game.

And to make it even more fun, the game has

built-in 'distractors' like doubt, fear and limiting be-
liefs, which will attack at random to test the player's
determination and perseverance.

FOCUS AND IT WILL GROW

One of the hidden truths of the game is that
whatever the player focuses on will grow in size and
intensity. Change the focus and 'life' will change.

That is to say, change the way he looks at things
and the things he looks at will change. In that way
he will attract that which he is.

Another secret is "Give and you shall be given,
seek and you shall find". So if the player wants
laughter in his game - the secret is to laugh, if he
needs help - go out and help someone else, if he
wants love – give love.

Give, give, give without any expectations - the
magic formula for success at all levels.

RECOMMENDATIONS

Should the player get bored and prefer to speed

up the evolution of the game, it is recommended that he makes a search for so-called hackers (spiritual teachers) who will share and give access to a lot of cracked code and other shortcuts (revelations).

Another good suggestion is to stick to accept, adjust and accommodate to whatever situation the player is confronted with, in combination with the following styles of playing:

- Non-violence
- Truthfulness
- Non-stealing
- Moderation
- Non-greed
- Do good - be good

Yet another good idea and point collector is to do as many perfect actions as possible: That means an action that hurts no-one, but gives some benefit to someone, the player himself included.

SICK LOGIC

Along the different levels, the player will be confronted by many indications of a sick logic affecting this illusionary 'world'.

In the words of writer Michael Ellner: "Everything is backwards, everything is upside down. Doctors destroy health, lawyers destroy justice, universities destroy knowledge, governments destroy freedom, the major media destroy information and religions destroy spirituality".

These signs of a twisted mentality ruling behind the scenes and guarded by the Black Angels are added purposely to help the player 'wake up'.

CHILL

Every 24 hours, the player needs to put his computer on standby (sleep) to avoid overheating the processors and, at the same time, 'defragment' the hard discs (dreaming).

If the player faces tiredness or exhaustion (for the body) it is recommended to amplify the intake of air (life force) or simply go out and help other players.

By giving a helping hand without expecting anything in return, the player automatically regains strength and inner power.

Once recharged, the computer needs to be re-booted (wake up) in order to be ready for another round (yet another day). The restarting of the PC can be done verbally (good morning) or by physical movement (stretching the body).

MOVING BACKWARDS

Should the player choose to neglect the recommendations, here are some signs to look out for (since they are sure indicators that the player is 'moving backwards'):

- Dis-ease
- Dullness
- Doubt
- Carelessness
- Laziness
- Sensuality
- False perception
- Failure to reach firm ground
- Slipping from ground gained

These indicators will be activated one-by-one in a long series if not stopped by the player.

The sooner he becomes aware of what is going on, the better.

Since most players aim at evolving, it is advisable to 'hang with the right crowd', meaning choosing fellow players among the ones more advanced than himself.

KEEP THE MEAT SUIT HEALTHY

To keep the computer (the body) in good condition, it is advisable to keep it clean and to avoid too many toxins, since this will clog up the system.

Instead, it is recommended to serve the body good fuel in the form of fresh vegetables, fruits and clean water.

DIS-EASE ~ YOUR FRIEND

It is also important to become aware of the mental state and the way of thinking, since looped fearful/hateful thought patterns may cause serious malfunctions in both mind and body.

It may even cause game over (Death).

So called dis-ease can also be caused by viruses or bugs leaking in through the fire wall (the body shell) sometimes causing serious damage to the player's system.

To avoid this, a special anti-virus program has been installed by default (the immune system), ensuring that the body's natural state is being supported by a wonderful self-healing process.

There are many different ways of handling disease. The clever player will be advised to carefully choose his way of looking upon 'bad health', since it is often a very powerful indicator of when he is moving in the wrong direction, off the track and back into fear.

AVOID KILLING

In this game everything is possible, even though it is not always recommended. One of the main things to avoid is killing other players (murder). This includes all types of living creatures, not only human beings.

Breaking this basic rule will cause difficulties in future games (bad karma).

In the same way, the more good deeds the player adds, old karma is dissolved and future games are made easier and smoother.

As mentioned before, the main ingredients in the game of life are based on cause and effect, a wonderful setting when used in combination with the random generator called free will.

Greatness courts failure and impatience robs the player of the pleasure of living into the anwers. So don´t worry, something wonderful is about to happen. Just keep the faith.

DEATH

Should the player decide to quit, this is possible, but will terminate the Personal Character once and for all (death).

If the player decides to go ahead, his body and mind will appear dead and lifeless to the other players, even though the player himself (the spirit) is 100% fine and just returns to the Source - until he decides to join the game again.

However, he now has to choose a new Personal Character. During this time-out period he can only contact other players through mediums or dreams, visions, and meditation.

ONLINE SUPPORT

The online support is available 24/7 and can be contacted through prayer, strong repeated thoughts or meditation.

The answers will mostly come in subtle form, meaning that the player needs to be very aware of hints and inner nudges – and then act on them.

TECHNICAL SUPPORT

The player also has access to a highly skilled technical support team (angels), which will happily assist whenever needed.

Only one rule applies: the angels are not allowed to interfere without being called.

NEVER LEFT THE SOURCE

One of the major aims of this game is to discover that the player actually doesn't need anything. She/He is, and always has been, totally free, immortal and connected to the Source.

Remember, everything changes and everything remains the same. Everything changes but everything returns, so don't be sad, be glad.

Signs of such higher understanding take the shape of hearing celestial music or visually decoding the matrix, thus making it possible to accomplish anything at all.

Once the code is cracked things like walking on water, going through walls, travel freely in space, turn water into wine and resurrect from the 'dead' is a piece of cake.

ALL IS ONE

And then, at the final level of understanding, the player will become aware that the Intelligence that created the game is actually the same intelligence with which he is thinking.

And that all the rest of the players are just other aspects of the same source.

Through the understanding that all is one, enlightenment follows and a wonderful feeling of total bliss is achieved. And then...

GAME OVER !!!

or is it...?

CREDITS

Having once completed the game scoring the highest points (saints), some players decide to join the game again, but this time to reveal the secrets to the rest of the players, or at least to the ones who are willing to listen.

This normally causes a great deal of problems to the Black Angels. At times these Black Angels will do anything to stop these leaks of truth, even commit horrendous acts of violence.

To make up for this added karma, and once the game is over, these Black Angels are thanked in a most deep and grateful way, since it is only the strongest of souls that voluntarily takes on heavy karma like murder – as selfless service with the aim of assisting other players to evolve spiritually.

PERSONAL NOTES

PERSONAL NOTES

ABOUT THE AUTHOR

Truth Seeker, Code Breaker and Peacemaker Ole Dammegard, awarded the Prague Peace Prize, and adopted by the Apache Nation, is an author, International speaker, former journalist, musician, artist and investigator, who has dedicated the last 35 years to researching many of the global conspiracies. Millions of viewers and listeners around the world have taken part of his interviews and presentations. His main focus has been to find out the truth about the assassinations of JFK, the Swedish Prime minister Olof Palme, Robert Kennedy, Martin Luther King, John Lennon and Lady Di, plus the terror attacks of 911, Norway, Oklahoma City and many, many more.

Ole has done some 500-1000 International interviews (with a total of several millions of views) and is now considered a leading expert on false flag operations and is believed to have managed to expose and stop several planned massacres. Ole has appeared as an International speaker in the USA, UK, Germany, the Czech Republic, Belgium, Holland, Denmark, Norway, Estonia, Poland, Gibraltar, Mexico, Spain and Sweden. He was chosen to represent the people of Europe when giving a JFK-memorial speech in Dealey Plaza, Dallas, Texas, on November 22, 2016, as well as being one of the speakers at the World Peace Day in Gibraltar.

He is an International Raja Yoga teacher and the author of four books, including what has been named a Master Piece; Coup d'etat in Slow Motion, Part I-II, as well as receiving awards for his air brush art work and custom car creation. In addition, as a young man he was quite an adventurer, who after having traveled alone on an old bicycle through Europe, helped to smuggle out some friends from war-torn Iran, beautifully described in the true story 'Shadow of Tears'.

Please contact Ole Dammegård by emailing info@lightonconspiracies.com.

Testimonials and Praise for Re-Mind Me

Reading 'Re-Mind Me' was an eye-opener - I can definitely say it's one of the most remarkable books I've ever read. I had browsed a lot through philosophy, meditation, alternative this, alternative that, but they somehow always seemed to look only at a fraction of human life.

Based on the author's acute observation of our current obsession with the pursuit of illusory goals, the book takes the reader on a journey exploring many of the motives and misconceptions which now inform our everyday lives. It was really refreshing to find a profound look at universal truths. The author has the stunning ability to go to the core of every issue. This is a must-read book for all those who believe in the ideal of making the world a beautiful and harmonious place to live in.

Gurinder Garg, Dexterous Technologies, India

- -

I received 'Re-Mind Me' on my birthday and I just tonight finally had the chance to run myself a hot bath and soak and read! I loved it! The author is obviously such a special soul and his little book is thought provoking and inspired.

Bruce Littlefield, Best-selling author and
TV-personality, New york, USA

Just finished reading the fabulous book 'Re-Mind Me' - in fact I read it twice as I was so intrigued at how cleverly it was written. It may be little but it sure packs a big punch. There aren't really any books out there on this subject that are written in such a way to be able to hold my children's attention, but this is one that will and I can't wait to get their reactions to it also.

Vanessa Woolley, Costa del Sol, Spain

'Re-Mind Me' is a very interesting look at our journey through life.

Bert Heaton, Director of Business Development,
Learning Strategies Inc, USA

'Re-Mind Me' - an awesome job!

Dr. Joe Rubino
The Center for Personal Reinvention, USA

What a fantastic read this is!!!!!!!!!! Jackpot!! Amazing and sooo funny tooo. I truly hope this will be a huge success!!!!!

Siva Trefzer, The Integral Yoga Centre, UK

I don't usually read stuff like this, I am a sceptic; but on this occasion I did and so glad I did. Yesterday I took time to read 'Re-Mind Me' - especially the bit about the player leaving the comfort zone and challenges faced from all directions forcing him back to the comfort zone and thought 'God that's happening to me!!!! So this morning as I set up my clinic with the usual butterflies and anxiety I called on the angels and told myself this to shall pass... over and over again. Today has been better for sure. I will try it again on Monday and again on Tuesday........ and see!

Julia Knight, UK

When I read the book the first time, I laughed laughed and laughed about the original way of describing our human 'mission' here. It is a great help to become the observer of yourself, and certainly not take this experience too serious. I only wanted to sit with the it for the rest of the day. I am so inspired and have started seeing with new eyes, tasted new flavours, and smelled new fragrances of life from reading this little/big book. I carry it in my bag. And guess what my friends and family are getting as a present! Peace and love filled with joy, laughter and light.

Dora / Devamani Fyllum, Denmark

Ole Dammegard has put this dynamic manual together to illustrate how life can be lived to its fullest. There is no judgment, no plan, just a road map to guide us to exist in this world with the highest spiritual understanding. His aim is to provide this wonderful knowledge to serve others who find the traditional approach too difficult to understand.

Ole has gone through the spectrum of life's obstacles and sufferings and has emerged not only unscarred or bitter, but full of love and gratitude. May this booklet serve many on their path to Self–realization. May many be inspired to live a spiritual life in this earthly body and fill the world with peace and joy.

Nalanie Chellaram, International Yoga Teacher,
Spain, Gibraltar, Hong Kong

- -

When I forget who I truly am, believing that I am separated and sometimes even abandoned, all alone, on my own, Re-Mind Me is a good companion. A friend softly whispering in my ear, letting me know that this is part of the game. The game I chose to play when I entered this world. Reminding me that I am the creator of my life, the one I have been waiting for - the Joy of rememberance who I am. I wish you every success with the Manual.

Malou Berg, International Singer, Sweden

- -

All seekers of the truth ought to read and absorb as much of 'Re-Mind Me' as they are capable of, since the simple explanations are of immense value and may be applied to the everyday situations that we all encounter in our lives. This book may indeed help to change the world by offering you a way to change your view of the world. So let us all re-mind ourselves and watch the world re-arrange itself. And please never forget that Love is more powerful than fear – always.

Bente D, Jewellery maker, Mallorca, Spain

- -

Busy schedules, every day full of activities, running around like 'headless chickens', running after things that don´t really exist or don´t really matter... I think we can all relate to that in some way... Now is the time to step back and Re-Mind ourselves with this fantastic little read, what is REALLY important in our lives; what really IS; who we are and why here. Brilliant, well done!

Mara Agnieszka, Poland

- -

I looked over the delightful, meaningful and amusing operating manual 'Re-Mind Me'. Very nice. You asked if you could help... you already are by sharing in your creative way the message of awakening. Thank you!

Daniel B. Holeman, artist Awaken Visions, USA

I read Re-Mind Me and enjoyed it so so much. It is clever, original and very thought-provoking and helpful. Congratulations.

Merle King, author of 'Silver and Time', UK

Divinely inspired, my spiritual teacher said. I can only agree one hundred percent. I have seen Ole write like this before, totally in-spirit (inspired) and letting whatever comes to him flow out on paper. This time this little book came and WOW, what a delicious gem. It makes you think, it makes you laugh, it makes you question life and the way we live from a totally new direction. A game manual for life, what a cool idea! Very entertaining and easy to read. Well done, my love.

Kim Kamala Ekman, Kamala's Yoga, Spain

Suosittelen, upea kirjanen - oikea 'Elämän pelin' manuaali! I can warmly recommend this to anyone!
Sari Penttila, Finland & Spain

Had another read through of 'Re-Mind Me' which I love. I'm already playing the game and as a ghost writer I find I have a sneaky advantage. During PLAY I already inhabit several other Personal Characters - but they chose me. Can't wait for GAME OVER when I get to choose my own!
Peter Brookes, author of 'Meeting Merigan', UK

I thought it was fun to see elements of the Yoga Sutras of Patanjali brought together in such a modern and light hearted manner, where its universal message is simplified in the form of a manual for the computer game of "Life". I think this original way of presenting it is a great way to reach those who haven't had a chance to read the traditional books, and re-minding everyone what its really all about.. Good luck with spreading the word!!
Sandra Sundberg, Brazil

We live in a world where children very quickly learn the basics of computers and adapt readily to the language associated with their functioning. Sadly we seem to have forgotten many of the concepts and ideas that can lead to us living fulfilled lives. 'Re-Mind Me' manages to draw the reader stage by stage into this 'mysterious' world using the well understood language of the millions who are so computer literate. Well worth a read for those who feel that life may be just a little more than a collection of situations 'crashing' with each other!

Mark Montovio
Founder of The JM Foundation, Gibraltar

- -

How do you succeed in the game of life? Who are the players? What are the obstacles? By becoming aware of oneself and following the guidelines of Ole Dammegård's manual to 'the game,' we can begin to understand our thoughts about our actions and ultimately win the game of life.

Ina Edelkraut
Founder of Friedensfestival, Berlin, Germany

- -

What an amazing book. It truly reflects how I feel about life in general.

Karen Fox, UK

'Re-Mind Me' is GOOOOOD!!!!

Kirsty Welles, Spain

'Re-Mind Me' is a great little book! It is written in way that it is fun to read and at the same time helps you to open your eyes and gives you practical tips on how to approach and deal with your life. The comparison of our lives with a computergame makes the messages very easy to understand for young people. A great little book to be put on your wishlist AND give list.

Rik Wiersema, the Netherlands

I'm gonna send 'Re-Mind Me' to a friend who is going through a tough crisis. Right away.

Vibe Schrøder, Denmark

'Re-Mind Me' is a fantastic read, very wise and entertaining.

Marion Devine, UK

- -

'Re-Mind Me' really makes you think...

Frans Meixner, Holland

Made in the USA
San Bernardino, CA
28 June 2020